15 Frequently Asked Questions To Consider Before Writing an eBook

GLENNYS MARSDON B.Psych

ISBN:
ISBN-13:

DEDICATION

To everyone who has come along to a workshop or one on one, and asked a curly question.

CONTENTS

PROLOGUE

In June 2010 I toyed with the idea of publishing an eBook. Like most tough decisions the initial phase was the hardest, with fear of the unknown stifling my ability to make rational decisions. Usually I'd turn to the latest research for guidance however, as with any technology in its infancy, the information was inconclusive and constantly changing. The question I faced was whether to wait until things settled down or jump in and learn along the way.

Six months later, I published an e-version of my first book, *50 Ways To Grieve Your Lover.* While not without its problems the initial experience was nowhere near as horrible as I'd imagined. Moreover, it was an absolute thrill to see my book listed on Amazon and incredibly heart-warming to receive a royalty cheque outlining sales from around the world.

Knowing that my little book may have helped widows in other parts of the world made by soul sing. The positive experience had me considering how else I could use the medium.

I should disclose that my background is in consumer psychology where I've spent over 20 years researching why we do the things we do. Hence, when faced with this question I drew on my research experience to investigate the world of e-Publishing. This included interviewing key publishers and attending as many e-Publishing seminars as I could find.

Two years later, things were still not perfect in the land of e-Publishing, and for some reason people started asking me for advice. After a while I decided to share what I'd learnt.

The result was an eBook called, *To E-Publish or not To E-Publish*.

Six years on, I now have nearly ten years' experience and have published around seven eBooks. It would've been more, but other work kept getting in the way.

More importantly, along the way I have experienced working with several e-Publishers. Some were good, others promised a long-term relationship but faulted soon after the honeymoon period ended.

As the technology keeps getting easier, more and more people keep asking for advice, and I now run courses on the subject.

Recently some students told me they couldn't find *To E-Publish or not To E-Publish* online. The file appears to have disappeared along with the e-Publisher. Hence, this current book represents an update of the original book.

The book contains some of the original research, as well as updates, as it's interesting to compare that with current day experiences. It must be stressed that this book does not contain all the answers. Nor am I a publishing expert. It's merely the outcome of nearly ten-years' experience. My hope is that the questions help shorten the decision process for you.

I wish you well in your writing life.

Glennys

Note:

Throughout the book we have referred to e-Publishing or 'electronic publishing'. This is to overcome spellcheck issues and to help demystify the name.

We have also settled on the term 'eBook' while some publications prefer e-book or ebook. This is to avoid spellcheck issues.

1 WHICH E-PUBLISHING PLATFORM SHOULD I USE?

The main question I get asked is which e-Publishing platform should I use?

People seem to think that if they pick "the right" e-platform this will guarantee them publishing success. While this is a legitimate question there are so many more important questions to ask, particularly if you aim to be in the writing game for the long haul. We'll cover these other questions in the coming pages, in the meantime let's get this one out of the way.

Usually when someone asks about e-Publishing platforms, this tells me that they've already decided to publish the book themselves.

I usually like to make them stop for a moment and answer the following initial challenge question ...

Which of the following best describes what you do when faced with an Ikea flat pack. Do you ...?

Open the box and launch in disregarding the instructions all together.

Take a cursory glance at the instructions and feel confident you can do it anyway, only to find you have six mismatched screws left at the end of the exercise.

Carefully read the instructions, lay out each item, and methodically set about assembling the item.

Meticulously read the instructions and after assembling the item, write to Ikea to point out an error in the terms and conditions.

Never buy from Ikea all your furniture comes fully assembled.

As with most things in life, there are two ways to approach e-Publishing. You can do it yourself or pay someone to do it for you. The decision usually depends on three things: Knowledge Time Money

If you answered "c" above, then read on about the type of electronic platforms available. For all other answers, you will be interested in the next section about working with others.

Electronic Publishing Platforms
Technological advances over the past eight years have made it even easier for people to go it alone when e-Publishing. The internet is full of information on electronic publishing platforms and DIY conversion options. If you don't believe me just google 'conversion tools' and see what comes up.

While I prefer not to recommend one approach over another, here are some interesting sites that have stood the test of time, so far. Some I have used, some I haven't.

Smashwords is a free electronic publishing service. It was one of the first to enter the market and hence a lot of us used this one before switching to

Amazon. www(dot)smashwords(dot)com

Amazon offers two platforms. Both are free to use. They are:

Kindle Direct Publishing or KDP as it is known. This is the platform I've used the most. www(dot)kdp(dot)amazon(dot) com

Createspace goes one step further to provide an on-demand printing service for paper books, CDs and DVDs. www(dot)createspace(dot)com

Two others that a lot of people have used are:
www(dot)lightningsource(dot)com
www(dot)lulu(dot)com

Many eBook authors started off by writing a blog (see question 13). The main platforms used for blogs are either Blogger [www(dot)blogger(dot)com] or WordPress [www(dot)wordpress(dot)com].
WordPress has a reputation of looking a little more professional than Blogger. Blogger is a nice easy platform to start on.
Other platforms I've heard of but don't have any experience with are:
www(dot)apple(dot)com/au/ibooks-author
www(dot)calibre-ebook(dot)com
www(dot)publicious(dot)com
www(dot)wattpad(dot)com

DIY Style Guides
Most electronic publishing sites offer comprehensive Style Guides. Unlike the Ikea

catalogue, you must slowly work through the guides when formatting your book.

Smashwords. Some people have found the Smashwords Guide user friendly, others not so much. I have a short attention span when it comes to pages of technical detail, so I must admit I found it a bit hard going.

I did however manage to publish one eBook using this system. I should also say that this was in 2010 so things have probably progressed a lot since then. Smashwords do offer fantastic support. The only reason I no longer use them is because Amazon KDP came along with an easier format.

Amazon Kindle Direct Publishing. I've used Amazon Kindle Direct Publishing several times now and found it extremely user friendly. The guide is very helpful. I would recommend you take notes along the way about the decisions you make, and any codes you enter. That way you can simply slot in the same information the next time you use it. They also provide a good service if you get stuck.

How long does it take to publish an eBook?

The longest part of publishing an eBook is writing the book. Once I have my book content finalised (that means edited and proofread) and the cover finished, it generally takes me half a day to work through KDP and publish the eBook. The first time might take you a day.

2 WHAT DO I NEED TO ASK AN E-PUBLISHER TO MAKE SURE I DON'T GET RIPPED OFF?

Let's say we've established you're not an Ikea kind of guy or gal. That you'd prefer to work with an e-Publisher, rather than go it alone.

The past eight years have seen an increasing preponderance of e-experts popping up. Trying to make sense of them all will soon have the 'men in white coats' measuring you up for the latest long sleeve wraparound jacket.

Over the years I've come across all manner of people calling themselves e-Publishing experts and professing to offer 'the ultimate solution'.

As in most professions it seems that the quiet guy beavering away in the corner, was a better bet than the one in the shiny suit yelling the loudest. Sometimes, as I persisted in asking more and more dumb questions, I realised my teenage nieces were more knowledgeable than some of the experts charging an exorbitant fee. Thankfully, most of the hit and run operators have already gone by the wayside.

My advice is, don't take the experts at face value. Ask questions, lots of questions, they aren't dumb, and a genuine expert shouldn't make you feel that they are.

Contract

If you do get someone else to do the work for you, make sure you have a clear contract where both parties know exactly, and I mean exactly, what is expected of them.

Remember that you are entering into a long-term contract, well hopefully. This is particularly important if it's going to involve money. It is critical to have a clear understanding from the beginning. Have I said that enough? Some of the things you'll need to check are:

What experience do they have?

Can you talk to the other authors on their books?

Do they have testimonials?

Can you check for changes in the final proof copy before the book goes online?

3 WHAT KIND OF HIDDEN FEES SHOULD I WATCH OUT FOR?

There are two parts to e-Publishing, converting your text into an eBook and publishing your book. Some electronic publishers do both parts, while others only focus on the conversion part. Make sure you know exactly which they are offering.

Some e-Publishers freely disclose what they charge for converting and then publishing your book. Make sure you know what the fees cover before your get started. For example, you should ask:

Is everything included in the quoted publishing cost or are there additional fees along the way?

What is the cost for converting the document to an eBook?

Does the fee include editing?

Is distribution (i.e. putting it up on Amazon etc.) included in the conversion cost or is this extra?

If publishing is separate, what sites are included in these costs e.g. Amazon, Smashwords any others?

GLENNYS MARSDON

4 HOW DO ROYALTIES WORK?

Royalties can be a grey area.

If you're going it alone, without an electronic publisher, and using a site like Amazon you won't have to worry about this. Amazon clearly states how much of a royalty you will receive. The amount varies depending on a few choices you make, but these are clearly explained on the site.

If you are using an e-Publisher, you'll need to check exactly what is involved when they talk about royalties. There are three elements to royalties:

The price the customer pays

The commission the distributor or publishing platform takes e.g. Amazon.

The commission the electronic publisher takes.

When an e-Publishers talks to you about their commission it's imperative to understand what this percentage is based on.

Is it a percentage of the original book price?

Or

Is it a percentage of the balance after Amazon has taken their cut?

Make sure all parties are clearly on what is involved.

Royalty Threshold

Aside from the actual dollar amount, it's important to know when royalties will be paid. Some publishers have a minimum threshold as this helps reduce their administration costs.

This is understandable given that some royalties amount to $1 or less. Make sure you check whether there's a minimum amount of sales you must reach before any royalties are paid.

Timing

Similarly, it is important to know if the payments will be made annually, quarterly or at another frequency. Whilst you may not be making a lot of money in the beginning it will grow, hopefully, and when it does it will directly impact your cashflow. It also means you can keep an eye on your relationship with your e-Publisher. Whether they've moved onto their next author and forgotten about you.

5 HOW MUCH SHOULD I CHARGE?

As soon as you mention e-Publishing the very next question after *'which platform should I use?'* is usually *'how much should I charge?'*

Price setting

As in traditional publishing when setting your price, you'll need to consider where you want your book to be positioned in the market place. Which strategy best fits you and your book. Would that be ...

High price/Low volume
Low price/High volume

One of the easiest ways to know what to charge is to go online and do some research.

This simple piece of research will ensure your book begins life with a sporting chance. As you sift through the books ask yourself ...

How much are similar eBooks retailing for?

What is the price differential between the e-version

and the paper version?

A couple of price examples identified during the initial research phase were:

Delabarre Publishing produces joke and travel books. They price them at $2.99, and at this price they sold 7,000 copies over 11 months, that's $20,930.

In the UK a single eBook from Mills and Boon hovered around the £3 to £5 mark, while a bundle of three books in the Vintage Mills and Boon edition were £15.

The book *Anything You Want* by Derek Sivers cost around $8, however it included the link to 200 downloadable songs (see question 11 for more details about this idea).

When I last used KDP (October 2018) they suggested a recommended price based on the type of book you were publishing, which was handy.

99 cents

You could put your book on for 99 cents, however I'd advise against it. Rightly or wrongly these books have been referred to as 'penny dreadfuls'. So, before you set your price consider the impact of this strategy on your brand. Do you really want to be included in the penny dreadful pile?

Free books

You can of course provide your book free of charge. There is absolutely nothing wrong with that, especially for a first-time author.

There's an interesting subculture of authors who offer their works completely free.

Perhaps you want to start a conversation about a

topic. Or maybe you just want to see if anyone will read your work and get some feedback on it.

Another segment that's latched onto this concept is the Business and Consulting market. So much so it's been suggested that the eBook may replace the business card in the future.

There are a number of sites offering free eBooks, for example:

www(dot)ebookdirectory(dot)com
www(dot)downloadfree(dot)pdf(dot)com

Timing and Cannibalisation

Another question is whether you should publish your eBook at the same time as the print version, if you're going to offer both. If you launch both at the same time, you're at risk of cannibalisation. Cannibalisation is particularly important if you're an established author, but also relevant to first-time authors. Would readers buy the cheaper e-version over the print version? If so is this a problem?

To some extent cannibalisation can be overcome through price and timing. For example, you could delay the launch of the eBook until after the traditional print book.

Alternatively, you could set the price of the eBook higher while the print version is being marketed. It could also be addressed by modifying the e-version, so it is slightly different to the print version. At present there doesn't appear to be a clear direction on this, so watch this space.

6 ARE THERE ANY PRIVACY OR COPYRIGHT ISSUES I NEED TO KNOW ABOUT?

Piracy is another area to consider. During my research I came across numerous references to Stephen King's early experience with electronic-publishing.

In 2000 King sold 400,000 copies of *Riding the Bullet* on the first day. Great right? But then the secure encryption was hacked. Thankfully things have progressed a lot since then.

If you aren't already aware, codes can be added to make it harder for eBooks to be copied or passed around. This comes under the DRM banner (Digital Rights Management). When you publish through Amazon you'll be asked if you want to use DRM or not.

So far, I have always chosen this option. My thinking is that after all the work you've put in, why would you risk someone stealing your work? Sure, the professional hackers will always be able to get around these things, but at least you can make it harder for them.

At the time of printing there was a healthy debate going on about whether this was worthwhile or not. Several organisations work on behalf of authors to keep abreast of these issues and I suggest you keep an eye on what they recommend. Three organisations to keep an eye on are:

The Australian Society of Authors
[www(dot)asauthors(dot)org]

CAL - Copyright Agency Limited
 [www(dot)copyright(dot)com(dot)au]

VISCOPY [www(dot)viscopy(dot)com(dot)au]

7 CAN I DO IT ALL MYSELF?

If you think you can do it all yourself, you're wrong. There are areas of electronic publishing that must be outsourced. According to internet marketing guru Seth Godin, electronic publishing cuts the publishing cycle by 90%. Consequently, the speed with which a book can get onto an eBook shelf is staggering. This also means that in the excitement of rushing to publish, important elements can get ignored.

You still need to enlist the services of a good editor and proof reader.

As my wonderful editor pointed out, you can't see your own errors, no matter how many times you read something, or how well you write.

Make sure you invest in a good proof reader, or two, and a good editor who understands your style.

8 HOW IMPORTANT IS AN EBOOK COVER?

As with traditional books a good cover design is paramount. This is the first impact your book has on the shelves. For eBooks this is even more important as the cover initially appears as a small thumbprint image. Hence the design must be crisp and powerful at the smallest level.

As e-Publishing has progressed there are several packages that can help with cover design.

Amazon offers a range of design assistance. When I first wrote this book I hadn't used this feature. However I've now used the Kindle Direct Publishing feature twice and found it excellent. It's so simple to use and produces a nice professional finish. You can use your own images of pick from a library supplied. Highly recommended.

Canva. This platform steps you through the design process. They also offer a wide range of templates. I've used this a couple of times but am yet to get the hang of it. www(dot)canva(dot)com

Fiverr. Through this site you can pay people $5 to design a cover for you. www(dot)fiverr(dot)com

Phoster. This app has 70 templates that help with book covers.
www(dot)bucketlabs(dot)net/portfolio/phoster/

Depending on how important the book is, it may be worth paying a design expert to make sure the cover looks professional and inviting.

For most of my eBooks I've made my own covers. This has involved sourcing images that are copyright free. I then use Power Point to build the image before converting it into a photo. I used this method because when I started my e-Publishing journey there wasn't anything around. It's suited my needs so far.

For this book I used the Create Space book cover designer. I and found it incredibly intuitive. I highly recommend it.

A couple of tips:

The cover represents you, so make sure it fits your brand.

The cover should look good in black and white as well as colour.

Any images used must be copyright free.

9 WILL E-PUBLISHING WORK FOR MY BOOK?

What style of book have you written? Is it a novel, a collection of poetry, or a picture book? Does it have text only or include photographs, drawings or diagrams? Is it a children's book?

Text

The e-Publishing platform works well for both fiction and non-fiction books that employ standard text without any fancy formatting or placement.

At the time of writing the initial book about e-Publishing, the medium was less kind to books requiring greater control over how the text appeared on the page. Things may have changed but I haven't experimented with that, so I can't be sure. Suffice to say, if you've written a book using text only, then e-Publishing is an appropriate medium. Otherwise you may need to do some further research.

Images

Similarly, at the time of writing the first book the medium wasn't ideal for books heavily reliant on pictures, images and diagrams.

Back then, it was difficult to find an eBook approach that placed text directly on top of an image, like in a children's book. At the time I tested this by downloading several free eBooks that included images. In most instances there was no guarantee where the image would fall on the page. Sometimes as you scrolled up the page the image would appear intact, other times it was split across two pages. This was a flaw in my first eBook, *50 Ways To Grieve Your Lover*, the technology simply wasn't ready then.

This may have changed by now. There was talk of an interesting iBook Authoring tool coming to market. If not, and if image placement is important in your book, then this is something you'd need to research further.

If not, then e-Publishing may not be ideal for image heavy books e.g. children's story books, high-end art books or photography books.

Aside from the technological consideration there's a bigger issue at hand for image heavy books. Do people want to look at these books on digital platforms? Think about your coffee table book. Do people really want to look at these images on a screen or do they prefer large A3 photographs?

Technical books

Another consideration is whether your book includes complex diagrams or flowcharts. They may not be ideal for small screens, even though readers can zoom in.

Timeliness

Time is another factor. Not the time it takes to get an eBook onto the shelves. No, we're talking about the timeliness of the content. Is your book at the cutting edge of technology? Could the information be out of date within six months?

Electronic books are an excellent solution for information that is rapidly changing. They can be quickly revised, updated and saved to another version.

More importantly readers who have purchased an earlier copy of an eBook, can be advised to download the latest version.

10 WHICH MARKETS RESPOND WELL TO E-PUBLISHING?

You may want to reconsider meandering down the electronic publishing path if you've written a book about, *100 Decorating Tips For A Bush Humpy*. The target market for this book may have already taken a left turn, and have no access to a shower, let alone a computer. In contrast eBooks have been shown to work extremely well in other markets. Below are a few examples.

Low vision/Older consumers

People with age-related macular degeneration and other forms of vision loss are being targeted with online games, puzzles and even online eye exercises.

The advantage of eBooks for these readers is they can adjust the text size accordingly.

It was also interesting to read that, when the Pew Internet & American Life Project investigated internet users over 50 years of age, they found that between April 2009 and May 2010 their social networking use had doubled from 22% to 42%. By 2018 the figures had increased to around 64% amongst 50 to 64-year olds and 37% for those over 65 years. Clearly this group is becoming more comfortable with technology. Given these findings, along with the ageing population, it would be unwise to ignore this segment.

Romance and Erotica

It's been well documented that romance and erotica books perform extremely well in the eBook market. A quick look at the Mills and Boon site would support this.

Aside from individual books, the site offers bundled eBooks in packs of two to ten different titles. They also include an online library.

Maybe eBook success in this market has something to do with their ease of digestibility and disposability. Or perhaps the writers have tapped into the publics' growing need for escapism during tough economic times. Then again maybe it's more superficial than that. Maybe it has something to do with being able to read a wide range of risqué books on an electronic device, where others can't see the cover … a bonus for teenage boys everywhere. Now that's something to contemplate on your next long-haul flight. Is that suited CEO type sitting next to you really reading a company report, I wonder?

The Travel Market

The e-platform has also become a favourite for travel guides. It's been well documented that frequent travelers have a fondness for eBooks. The main benefit being that they can have a stack of books at their fingertips. A book for every mood, and let's face it there are a lot of moods when travelling.

Business Markets

Apart from our frequently travelling CEO with his secret penchant for porn, the business market is also primed for eBooks.

During his time in office, President Obama directed government agencies to digitize their archives. This was so the public could have better access to information in the future.

Several articles have been written about consultants using eBooks to leverage their business. These people use eBooks to: profile their experience; launch theories; generate discussion; engage prospective clients and add value to core services.

Polarising or Embarrassing Topics

As stated earlier, eBooks enable people to read in secret. So, if your book touches on a delicate topic that polarizes the population, e-platforms may provide an opportunity to increase your readership.

Geographical considerations

Another consideration is the geographical spread of your potential readership. If most of your target market is confined to a small local township then a small traditional print run may be appropriate.

However, if you envisage your book having a wider reach say nationally or internationally, and who doesn't, then eBooks are an invaluable distribution tool.

Placing your book on Amazon instantly opens a world of readers, and it's fascinating to see your quarterly sales figures broken down by country. Think about how much harder it would be to market your book internationally through traditional means. Would it even be possible without the support of a traditional publisher, agent or overseas distributor?

So, before wading further into the e-river ask yourself these questions about the target market for your book:

Does your target market have access to a computer?

Would they want to read your book onscreen or are they married to traditional print?

If yes, keep going. If not turn around and return to the shore.

11 WHAT OTHER TYPES OF ELECTRONIC PUBLISHING COULD I USE?

We've thought about who your target market is, and the type of book you're writing, now let's think about how your readers might like to access your work. Sure, your book could be read on Kindle, iPad or on PC, but what about some other ideas for electronic content delivery?

Audio Books

In the past audio books were deemed persona-non-grata unless you were silver-haired and living in a nursing home. This is no longer the case. Two changes in society have impacted on our attitudes towards audio books.

First, numerous consumer psychology reports point to people becoming more cocooned and isolated in their homes. Added to this, the ageing population and rising number of single households has seen increasing rates of loneliness and depression.

While social media sites like Facebook are helping address these issues, so too are audio books. It's been found that a story read in soothing tones can help combat loneliness.

Secondly as our lives move at a faster pace, many people lament the lack of time to sit and read a book. Indeed, for many the activity has become a privilege. New technology means books can now be accessed while on the move.

In 2007 independent research undertaken by Lewis and Clark Research found a 6% increase in audio book sales. They also suggested that technological advances, such as audio book download subscription services, would see this trend continue to rise.

In addition, being able to download a book, rather than buy it on CD, led to better pricing. The researchers found that downloads had grown to 21% of the audio book market. They further suggested that with the high proportion of high school students carrying portable audio players, it would make sense to publish textbooks in audio formats in future.

Similarly, the AAP (Association of American Publishers) reported an increase in domestic audio book sales of 3.5% in 2009. In 2015 downloaded audio book sales continued to increase, in fact they'd doubled in popularity since 2012.

They were the fastest growing format (a growth of 37%), had reached double figures, and accounted for $159 million in 2015.

A recent google search revealed a whole subculture of audio books.

This included audio book clubs, audio book gift clubs, audio book club collections. Some of the sites for audio books were:

www(dot)audioeditions(dot)com
www(dot)audiobook(dot)com(dot)au
www(dot)simplyaudiobooks(dot)com

Going onto sites like these you will see names like James Patterson, Janet Evanovich, Agatha Christie and Harry Potter to name a few. The books can be purchased or rented.

Would your book work well as an audio book? Taking the audio book path could open a whole new market.

Multimedia

Electronic publishing also provides a world of multimedia possibilities. Books are already being enhanced with things like music links, videos and other research material. Just a few of the examples uncovered during my research were:

An Italian cookbook produced with musical accompaniment;

A romance novel with a tango lesson video;

A crime novel with blueprints of the building being robbed;

Travel books with links to brochures;

Fiction books with a video introduction from the author.

In another example Seth Godin launched one of his Domino Project eBooks, *Anything You Want* by Derek Sivers. The book included a code for downloading 200 free songs from indie musicians that had been hand-selected by the author.

Apps

These days content needn't be delivered via a

book. What about an App? Would your book reach more people it if was an easy to download App?

Instalments and e-newsletters

Alternatively, you could publish your book through a dedicated website where readers subscribe and receive a chapter at a time. Perhaps the chapters could be sent as a series of e-newsletters.

Before you reject this idea outright, it would be wise to remember that Charles Dickens began by distributing his stories as serials. Similarly, every month Mills and Boon offer a free read. They put up a chapter every two to four days.

So, maybe take a moment to think outside the square.

Could your book benefit from being in another format?

A Podcast perhaps?

Being different would certainly help you stand out from the crowd.

12 HOW WILL E-PUBLISHING IMPACT ON MY PERSONAL BRAND?

Regardless of where you agree with marketing or not, or whether you offer your work for $500 or free of charge, as someone trying to get others to read their work, you have a brand. A brand that needs to be managed.

Personal branding begins in childhood. By the time we reach high school we've already started to cement our brand position. Were you the cool dude sitting in the back of the classroom dazzling your peers with your rapier wit? Or were you the teachers' pet jumping to their defence when it looked like a breakdown was imminent? No? Well perhaps you spent your lunchtime in the library fossicking amongst the shelves for T S Eliot?

Either way your brand was already forming. Every major life decision you've made since then has added to your brand. Whether you married, had children, remained single, lived in flat or an ashram. People formed a perception of you.

The question is …

Do you already have a strong market presence as writer, or other means? If so, what impact would e-Publishing have on this brand? Would it help or hinder the public's perception of you and your work?

Brand Attributes

If you're a first-time author, you're in the enviable position of being able to start your author brand from scratch. It's not often you get to do that.

How do you want to be portrayed in writing circles?

What attributes are important to you?

To help you decide, think about some of your favourite authors. How would you describe their brand? Do you want to be considered humorous, thought provoking, intelligent, ditsy, respected, feared etc.?

These questions are relevant for established authors too, as entering the e-platform enables them to refine their current brand.

Personal branding is a whole other topic, and one I will be addressing in another book in the future. In the meantime, consider the following …

Long term brand development

Strong brand development takes time. Consider this …

Whether a first-time or established author, how do you see your brand developing over time?

How important is it for you to be considered modern or up to date?

If you imagine positioning yourself as a hip artist in touch with the world around you, then there's no decision to be made, you need to enter the electronic publishing market. Not to do so would be detrimental to your brand.

Alternatively, maybe you prefer to be considered a technophile, a recluse. Maybe you've cultivated the cool of a bush poet. If so an e-Publishing presence may not be as important.

What would your readers expect?

What about your readers? What would they expect of you? Would they want you to have an e-platform? Are your readers at the forefront of technological change? Are they riding around on Segways, listening to music on their iPhones which camping out at Apple Stores waiting for the next release? Or are they traditionalists who view all e-authors just a smidgeon above kitten stranglers? How would they view your presence in the electronic publishing space?

e-Peers

Entering the e-Publishing market also means you're aligning yourself with the full spectrum of writers. From award winning authors to bloggers and fanfic writers. Would that thought keep you awake at night?

Don't be too hasty to answer that. Before you discard fanfic writers it would pay to do some research into that realm. It may surprise you to know that Joanne Harris, of *Chocolat* fame, recently revealed that she'd spent three years searching online communities. While doing so she wrote under a pseudonym seeking feedback on her story. Can you imagine reading her fanfic and commenting on it, only to find out later that you had been making suggestions to Joanne Harris?

So, how will entering the electronic publishing market impact on your brand?

As long as the move doesn't adversely affect your brand it's a wise decision from a marketing perspective.

13 DO I HAVE TO DO MY OWN MARKETING?

We've already mentioned several marketing related issues, here are four more to consider.

Marketing skills

How good are you at talking about yourself? Do you enjoy talking yourself up or does that thought send you into a hyperventilating huddle on the floor? Could you see yourself marketing the book?

Just like self-publishing, e-Publishing means you'll be doing your own marketing. Thankfully while the days of standing on the street corner dressed as a chicken are fading, it's not enough to just put your book online and expect the audience to come. At the very least you will need an online presence.

Thankfully there are several free marking guides online that can help you. However, while they provide a myriad of ideas, they are not the panacea. There is no one solution other than a lot, and I mean a lot, of hard work.

Online presence

As discussed earlier marketing will be considerably easier if your name is already known. Do you already have a readership base? If so it's a matter of replicating your traditional marketing efforts online.

At least now it's far easier to build your own brand online. At the most basic level it's as simple as opening a Facebook Author account.

No, that doesn't mean uploading your Christmas photos, unless of course your book is about Christmas. A Facebook Authors page must be treated like a professional business page.

This is the subject of another workshop and book, so I will leave it there for now.

Beyond a Facebook Author page is the author website. This can be as simple or complex as you like, just make sure it reflects your brand. If you want more information about what goes into an authors website just contact me (details at the end of the book).

Blog

Some people think having a blog is even worse than publishing an eBook. However, a blog is a brilliant way to build up a profile.

It's also a great way to build a readership base. Once you have established a relationship with your reader, and have their details, you have a great database for future promotions. The trick is to put the effort into making your blog worthwhile and this takes time.

It's also important not to abuse the relationship by bombarding your readers with emails and offers.

There are several sites that allow you to quickly develop a blog. As stated earlier the main two are Blogger and WordPress.

So, the real question is, are you up for the marketing challenge? For it will be a challenge, that's for sure.

14 HOW WILL TRADITIONAL PUBLISHERS REACT?

First-time authors often worry that if they self-published their book they'll make themselves persona-non-grata amongst traditional publishers. Moreover, they worry that, heaven forbid their book takes off, they'd be unable to approach traditional publisher in the future.

Over the past few years I've been fortunate to sit in on several pitches to traditional publishers. It was interesting to note that when a self-published book had been successful the traditional publishers were very impressed. While they were not interested in the current book the author had self-published, they were interested in others the author had in the pipeline.

Obviously, this may not hold true for all publishers, but it was interesting. You'll need to research each of the publishers you're considering approaching to gauge their views on this one.

What's happening in the publishing market?

In this instance I'll let the figures do the talking.

The July 2009 Association of American Publishers (AAP) figures showed that, domestic net sales included $16.2 million for eBooks sales. This represented a 23.5% increase for July and 173.9% for the year to date. [Note: This does not include eBooks offered exclusively through Amazon Publishing, Kindle Unlimited or self-published on Amazon].

In 2011 according to a website called www(dot)bookpublishingsoftware(dot)com

HarperCollins eBook sales accounted for 19% of sales in the USA and 11% of sales worldwide.

Likewise, Harlequin digital sales accounted for 13.6% of revenue, while for the Hachette Book Group the figure was 22%. In addition, Simon & Schuster digital sales accounted for 18% of revenue for the first quarter. That year, Amazon announced they were selling more eBooks than print books.

I appeared that in 2012 most traditional publishers did not want to be left out of the digital market. Public desire for eBooks could not be ignored. Indeed, some traditional houses published both the print and eBook versions simultaneously while others split the publication timelines. Other traditional publishers went further and split their whole business into two separate divisions - traditional versus online. Clearly eBooks were being taken seriously.

By 2015 the Pew Research Centre reported that 72% of Americans had read a book, or part of a book, in the past 12 months. This represented a decline from 76% the previous year. In contrast they reported that eBook readership had remained steady (27%: compared to 28%).

Similarly, figures from Book Publishing Software suggested that eBook market share had stabilised at 30% of sales. This echoes figures from Penguin Random House, where eBook sales accounted for 25%.

However, according to the AAP, eBook sales figures fell 11%. It should be noted that this was against a flat market that reported a 2% sales decline overall.

It should also be remembered that these figures did not include eBooks published exclusively through Amazon. They noted that across all book types, sales were down for Higher Education, PreK-12 course materials and Religious Presses. Whereas most of the decline in eBooks came from Children/YA genres.

Looking to the future, according to website www(dot)statistica(dot)com revenue from eBook sales in the US is expected to grow at an annual rate of 3.8%, resulting in $88 million by 2022.

This is supported by Amazon who recorded a 4% growth in eBook sales between 2015 and 2016. (Amazon accounts for the bulk of eBook sales e.g. 83% in the US).

While these figures are interesting and suggest eBooks cannot be ignored, that also highlight that we still don't have a comprehensive figure for eBooks sales. This is in part because independently published eBooks do not require an ISBN. In addition, the 2015 figures were also influenced by the adult colouring book phase and increases in eBook pricing structures.

We do know however, that more and more people who are reading eBooks are doing so on their phone e.g. an increase from 24% to 54% between 2012 and 2015 according to a US Nielsen survey.

Thus, these findings point to an immediate future where people will still be interested in reading eBooks, most likely on their mobile devices.

Know your digital rights
Given the changing marketplace it will be important for established authors to make sure they understand the digital rights of their back catalogue.

If you need help with this, The Australian Society of Authors is a good site for advice.

Other providers to watch
If you are interested in keeping abreast of the electronic publishing industry, I'd recommend watching key retails such as Dymocks to see what they do.

Similarly, a person to watch is Seth Godin who has experimented with different ways of publishing his works. At the end of a year-long experiment he concluded that ...

This (eBooks) is the most disruptive thing to happen to books in four hundred years. It's hard for me to see significant ways traditional book publishers can add the value they're used to adding when it comes to marketing eBooks. Unless they get busy convincing would-be buyers to give them permission to sell (e.g. through subscription databases).

It's an interesting thought.

So ... at present traditional publishers appear to have a foot in both camps.

One thing is for sure, if your book is a success without their input, rest assured they will take notice of you in the future.

15 DO I HAVE THE RIGHT PERSONALITY?

While the previous questions are important I'd like to suggest there's one question that overrides everything.

Do I have the right personality for e-Publishing?

How much of a risk taker are you?

Can you cope with uncertainty?

Do you like learning as you go?

When people find out I've entered the world of e-Publishing they have one of two reactions. Some turn their backs and caste me out to the bowels of literary hell while acknowledging the recent sale of my soul.

Others inch closer attempting to glean some powerful e-gem through osmosis.

In the end both groups sheepishly enquire about "the solution".

I usually feel that my reply leaves them disappointed. I'm sure most think I know "the secret" and am just not telling them.

The truth is that during my research I didn't find any mention of an overall industry-wide solution, apart from some comments about DRM, e-pub versions and open eBook specifications, and even these weren't without speculation. Just like the old days of Beta versus VHS videos the Holy Grail is still being crafted. Naturally there is an element of risk if you decide to jump in when the technology is still emerging, however it's also very exciting.

Therefore, your first decision comes down to two choices – the red or the blue pill. Either pick an e-Publishing path, dive in and see where it takes you, or keep waiting for the Holy Grail to be uncovered, and waiting, and waiting.

CONCLUSION

Eight years and around six eBooks later, I've reached the conclusion that traditional and electronic publishing complement each other.

If you take the time to consider these questions and don't rush in, I can highly recommend e-Publishing.

What will it be for you?

Will you dive in or stay sitting on the shore?

If you're still unsure I'd recommend a gentle approach. Rather than launching into e-Publishing with your life's work, make your first venture with a less important book and see how that goes.

I hope this information has been of some help. I'd love to hear how you go. Feel free to contact me through one of my social media platforms.

Good luck.

ABOUT THE AUTHOR

Glennys's passion for people saw her qualify as a psychologist in the 1980s, then spend nearly 30 years studying consumer behaviour.

Through her independent consumer psychology consultancy, *The Customers' Voice*, she's helped numerous organisations develop marketing plans, advertising campaigns and new products. She's also delved into a wide range of social issues, from the youth drug culture to domestic violence, family caring and retirement. All of this has enabled her to interact with a diverse range of people, a need that grew out of her first job with the Australian Red Cross where she spent three years travelling around Western Australia.

While at the Australian Red Cross she was responsible for the *Youth News* magazine, which went out to all West Australian schools.

In 2007 she published her first book, *50 Ways To Grieve Your Lover,* which was taken up by counsellors working in the Victorian Bush Fires and New

Zealand Pike Mine Disaster. As a result, she was profiled in a book by American internet and marketing guru Seth Godin in his book was called *Tales of the Revolution: True Stories About People Making A Difference.*

Due to the success of her first book she started a blog called *The Ponder Room* which attracted an international audience across 20+ countries after just six months.

In 2008 she wrote her first piece of fiction '*A Whales Tale*', which won first prize in the Stirling Literary Awards. This led to more freelance writing including a column in *MX5 Magazine*, a monthly column in *Swan Magazine* (since 2014) and regular gigs with on and off line magazines including, *Visit Perth City, So Perth, Tweet Perth, The Weekly Review* (Melbourne), *Divine* (Disability) and *ABC Ramp It Up* to name a few.

In 2010 she received the Rigby Award for services to cartooning due to her work on the Michael Collins Caricature Award, which was established to honour her partner. Running for four years it raised funds for the Heart Foundation.

In 2012 she was nominated for a Telstra Business Women's Award, and in 2013 her second book *Me Time 100 Strategies For Guilt Free Me Time*, landed her a People's Choice Award.

She currently spreads her time between freelance research, writing jobs, sitting on several government and nongovernment advisory Boards. As well as conducting workshops and mentoring sessions, covering topics such as …

Personal Branding;

Consumer Psychology

Writing Your First Book;

Overcoming Grief;

Gaining Guilt Free Me Time.

Other Books by Glennys

50 Ways To Grieve Your Lover: 100 Tips Gaining Back Control

Me Time: 100 Strategies For Guilt Free Me Time.

To E-Publish or not To E-Publish.

Freelance Life: An Action Plan To Help You Become A Successful Six Figure Freelancer

A Bouquet of Love (short story in this Anthology)

All Wrapped Up (short story in this Anthology)
Pondering About Series

Wit and Wisdom: Essays From The Most Isolated City In The World.

For more information go to
www(dot)glennysmarsdon(dot)com